M000250044

Copyright © by Harcourt, Inc.

Requests for permission to make copies of any part of the work should be addressed to School Permissions and Copyrights, Harcourt, Inc., 6277 Sea Harbor Drive, Orlando, Florida 32887-6777. Fax: 407-345-2418.

HARCOURT and the Harcourt Logo are trademarks of Harcourt, Inc., registered in the United States of America and/or other jurisdictions.

Printed in Mexico

ISBN-13: 978-0-15-352755-5
ISBN-10: 0-15-352755-2

1 2 3 4 5 6 7 8 9 10   050   11 10 09 08 07 06

Harcourt
SCHOOL PUBLISHERS
Visit *The Learning Site!* www.harcourtschool.com

Producers and Consumers

People provide goods and services.
Goods are things that people make or grow.
Services are work people do for others.
Consumers buy goods and services.

consumer

Goods and services can be bought and sold.
People who grow or make goods are called
producers.

Reading Check (Focus Skill) **Categorize and Classify**
What is the difference between goods
and services?

producer

Goods

Goods

Wanda Montañez

Wanda Montañez is from Puerto Rico. She moved to the United States as a young girl. She was proud to be from Puerto Rico. She wanted to wear clothes that showed how proud she was.

Wanda Montañez made her own clothes.

Montañez decided to make her own clothes. She makes clothes that have Spanish words on them. Her clothes help her show how proud she is.

1970

2030

1973 Moves to the United States with her family

2003 Starts her clothing company

Work and Income

People get income for making or selling goods or services. **Income** is money that people earn. They can use the money to buy the things they want or need.

An **occupation** is the work that people do to earn money. People often choose work they enjoy.

Reading Check (Focus Skill) **Categorize and Classify** What are some ways to earn income?

Occupations

builder

park ranger

At the Factory

Some people work in a factory. They make goods. They use **raw materials.** Wood is a raw material. It is used to make bats.

Wood is used to make bats.

cutting

branding

People in a factory use capital resources to do their work. Machines are one kind of capital resource.

Reading Check (Focus Skill) **Categorize and Classify**
How are raw materials used?

Machines are used to package bats.

sanding

packaging

How Much and How Many?

Sometimes too many people want to buy a good. There are not enough of that good for everyone. That good is **scarce.** Bad weather can make farm goods scarce.

Bad Weather

drought

flood

The prices of scarce goods go up in the marketplace. Goods are bought and sold in a marketplace.

Why do prices go up in the marketplace?

Blueberries can be bought at the marketplace.

Barter and Trade

Some people **barter** for goods. They give one thing to get another. They do not use money.

Bartering began long ago.

People in different countries **trade** goods and services. They buy and sell using money. Traded goods move around the world. They go on trucks, ships, and planes.

Reading Check Who trades goods and services?

Trade with the United States

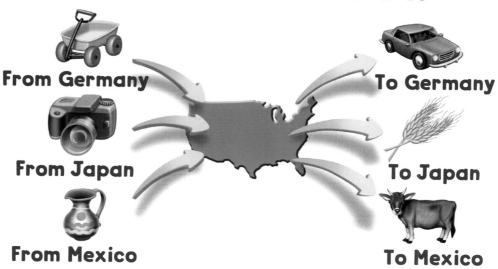

From Germany

From Japan

From Mexico

To Germany

To Japan

To Mexico

Activity 1

Match the word to its meaning.

goods   occupation   scarce

producers   raw materials   barter

income   trade

1. money that people earn
2. when there is not enough
3. to give one thing to get another
4. things that people make or grow
5. workers who grow, make, or sell products
6. to buy and sell
7. work that people do to earn money
8. a resource used to make a product

14

Activity 2

Look at the list of words. Put the words in a chart like the one below. Then use a dictionary. Learn what the words mean.

producer

goods

services

business

consumer

factory

occupation

income

free enterprise

want

raw material

human
resource

capital

resource

scarce

marketplace

manufacturing

trade

barter

		I Know	Sounds Familiar	Don't Know
	producer	✓		
○	goods	✓		
	services			✓
	business		✓	

Categorize and Classify Which is a raw material?

   tree   saw mill   lumberjack

1. **Vocabulary** What is the difference between goods and services?
2. What is a consumer?
3. What happens to the price of scarce goods?

Activity

Describe a Job Write about a job in your community. Does the job make a good or provide a service?